MW00954554

CHRIST
THE
SERPENT

Ancient African Mystery Series

Ainsworth Forgenie

Published by Kosmic Publishing

.

Contents

Introduction

Concealed within the pages of the bible is a treasure trove of sacred knowledge locked away from the casual gaze of the ignorant masses. Those who will be "ever seeing but never coming to a knowledge of the truth."

As the bible indicates these gems are revealed only to the wise and discerning, the mature. Those who are able to digest meat. Those who are willing to sell all they possess in order that they may of its succulence partake.

The rest are forever babes, suckling from the breast of those who peddle illusions. Illusions based on fear; inadequacy and dependency.

This work, which is the compilation of a series of articles, is an attempt to expose the reader to the Divine essence within, as against that which is without. Bringing to the fore the true meaning of the statement: The kingdom of heaven is within.

Do enjoy and share with those who you believe are able to digest its truth.

CHAPTER
1

Awakening Christ Consciousness

The Rebellion

On their way to the promised land, the children of Israel became weary and began to complain. They longed for the 'good old days', the days of their servitude in Egypt. Somehow, the memory of those days which they once dreaded became nostalgic. They forgot about the many arduous hours which they were required to work each day.

Lost to their memory was the demanding deadlines. They somehow also lost the remembrance of the many beatings when those deadlines were not met. Even the slaying of their offspring was somehow magically erased.

Instead, they chose to reflect on the good things like the food In particular the tasty, light bread which was their staple. And yes, the water – they had water. It was definitely not like it is now, where they are unable to quench their thirst.

The bible says that God took offense and attacked them with venomous serpents. Realizing their misdeeds, they repented and asked to be forgiven. What is God's solution to the dilemma?

Meditate On The Serpent

What else but the obvious, he commands them to look to the serpent on a pole for their healing. Now is it not passing strange that in a book where the serpent is seemingly demonized, that it should be their only avenue of deliverance? Why would God instruct them to do this? Especially when the word 'looked' used in verse 9, does not mean to glance casually upon. Rather, it means: *to look intently at.*

In other words, Moses was instructing them that their deliverance was predicated on them meditating on the serpent in order that they might receive their healing. Meditate on a snake? Would that not, at the very least be idolatry, but even worst *Satanic worship*?

The Serpent Healer

8 'The Lord said to Moses, "Make a snake [saraph] and put it up on a pole; anyone who is bitten can look at it and live." 9 So Moses made a bronze snake [nachash] and put it up on a pole. Then when anyone was bitten by a snake and looked at the bronze snake, they lived.'

Throughout history the serpent has, and still is, not just the giver of knowledge, but the healer. The serpent is the healing energy. It is the healing energy within. The Apostle Paul in Galatians 4:24 tells us that these are not historical events, rather they are allegories. That is, they are stories which reveal a hidden meaning and are not to be taken literally.

To stare at the serpent at the top of the pole, is the equivalent of meditating on the Pineal Gland. The serpent being equated to your activated Third Eye. Where is the Pineal Gland? It is located in the center of your brain. In the east, it is called your crown chakra. The Yoruba calls it your ori. So, you are being informed that the Pineal Gland/Third Eye is activated through meditation. Remember the story has nothing to do with anything outside of yourself – it is all about you. It is about **awakening the Christ within.**

The Egyptian Christ

Christ says:

'As Moses lifted up the serpent in the wilderness, even so must the Son of Man be lifted up'

Here the Christ is being equated with the serpent on the pole. Why? Because it is one and the same. The concept of the Christ predates the Jesus personality portrayed in the New testament. In fact, it can be traced all the way to the mystery schools of ancient Egypt. The original word was Krestos, its esoteric meaning was fire and is the equivalent of the Sanskrit word *Kundalini*. It is from the Egyptian Krestos that the Greek got Christos, from which we have Christ.

The Krestos/Christos is a state of consciousness. An advanced, awakened state of consciousness. It is an awakening of the Divinity within. The

Christ for thousands of years was never regarded as a single individual – any *one* person. It only moved from being a state of consciousness to a singular being, thanks to Rome.

CHAPTER
2

Serpents Above God's Throne

Previously, we looked at the allegory told in the book of Numbers. In that narrative, God instructed Moses to put a serpent on a pole and have the children of Israel meditate on it so that they might be healed. The word used in Numbers 21 for the serpent is saraph or Seraphim. Saraph as we discussed before means fiery serpent. Now in the scriptures, serpents represent fire and fire is associated with revelation and light.

When we activate the Pineal Gland, we are connecting with our divinity. We are opening ourselves up to the divine mind asleep within. Knowledge, otherwise concealed, becomes available to us. That which is invisible to the physical eye, or that which cannot be experienced through any of our five physical senses becomes accessible to us. We are illuminated.

Fiery serpents therefore represent higher consciousness. It is the activated Pineal Gland or Third Eye, It equates to the resurrection of the Egyptian Kristos which became the Greek's Christos - Christ consciousness.

Serpents/Seraphim Above The Throne

"Above him (yehôvâh) were seraphim, each with six wings: With two wings they covered their faces, with two they covered their feet, and with two they were flying.' **Isaiah 6:2**

Saraph is the word which God uses when he instructs Moses to put the serpent on the pole. Where do we find these Seraphim - fiery serpents? We discover them above the throne of God. *"Above him (yehôvâh) were seraphim..."* Now can you explain to me what God would be doing with serpents above his throne?

The very being, which is associated with nothing less than the devil itself, is covering the Holy One of Israel? Surely something's not right there, you would think. Of course, it is not, only if you refuse to look at it as it truly is – an allegory.

Your Kundalini Experience

Now remember that the throne of God (who is the king) can only reside in His kingdom. Where is God's kingdom? It is inside of you. According to the bible you are the kingdom. So where is the throne that Isaiah stands before? It is within – not without.

Isaiah in this story represents you. You are, through meditation, transported to a sacred space where your mind is illuminated. The Seraphim represents your awakening experience. But is there another way that we can know that the Seraphim represents you, and not a physical serpent? Yes, we know they are representative of you because it is described as having six (6) wings.

Numerology plays a key role in interpreting sacred literature. It is one of the mediums through which knowledge is concealed. Six is the number of man, it represents man. So, the six (6) wings, two (2) wings are used for flying, are describing your ascension. With your physical eyes covered and your feet at rest, you can now focus on seeing with your inner eye – your third eye. It speaks not of an external event. But rather your own divine experience. Or as the easterners would describe it – your Kundalini moment.

.

CHAPTER

3

Dark Sayings In The Bible

In the book of Genesis Chapter 3, we are introduced to the serpent in the bible for the very first time. Here its portrayal is not generally considered a complimentary one. In fact, it is one in which he is fingered as the one who is responsible for introducing sin into the world of mankind. Is it possible however that there could be another way of looking at this interaction between man and the serpent? Could this perhaps be one of the *dark sayings* found in the bible?

The Knowledge For The Masses

Before we take a look at an alternate view. Let it be here stated that in all religions there are two separate and distinct sets of knowledge. The first is what is referred to as exoteric knowledge, this is the 'knowledge' that is feed to the masses as truth. It is, that which is shared with those whom it is believed are either not capable of or worthy to receive the 'true knowledge'.

Jesus of course knew this. When his disciples asked him why he spoke to the people in parables and not clearly, he replied:

"Because the knowledge of the secrets of the kingdom of heaven *has been given to you, but not to them."*

Here Jesus is openly acknowledging to his selected few, that there is truth that is not to be shared with the masses. There is occult (meaning secret not evil) knowledge which is only to be shared with a select few. There are things that, it is believed, the masses either do not have the capacity to grasp, or are not worthy to receive or both.

He further goes on to clarify by stating:

"Whoever has will be given more, and he will have an abundance. Whoever does not have, even what he has will be taken away from him..."

In other words, those with expanded minds will be given more. The more the mind is opened, the more knowledge will be dispensed. On the other hand, true knowledge will be withheld from those whose minds/eyes are forever closed. It is based on the principle that *"you do not cast your pearls before swine, or give that which is holy (unique, different) to..."*

The Knowledge For The Selected Few

The second type of knowledge is referred to as esoteric knowledge. Esoteric refers to that which is to be shared exclusively with a comparatively small group of people – the chosen few. Christ spoke to three groups of people:

1. Firstly, he addressed the masses/the crowds.
2. Secondly, he spoke to the (120) one hundred and twenty.
3. Thirdly, he shared exclusively with the (12) twelve.

The only group he shared the meaning of the parables to were those belonging to the third group – the twelve (12). To these he shared the secrets; the mysteries of the kingdom; *the dark sayings.*

The Dark Sayings

What are *dark sayings*? *'Dark sayings'* refer to the knowledge taught in the ancient mystery schools. These schools can be traced all the way back to ancient Egypt. It was in these schools that the *'sacred knowledge'* was shared with the chosen few. This knowledge was shared though parables; riddles; puzzles and hard questions.

In the bible there are many references to these *dark sayings.* The bible is actually a collection of *dark sayings* passed along throughout the ages.

In Psalm 78:2 it says:

"I will open my mouth in a parable: I will utter dark sayings of old..."

The book of Proverbs 1:6 tells us that the purpose of the book is to give to the diligent/the seeker the ability:

'To understand a proverb, and the interpretation; the words of the wise, and their dark sayings."

Referring to the wisdom of Solomon we are told, "*...when the queen of Sheba heard of the fame of Solomon, she came to prove Solomon with* **hard questions** (*dark sayings*) *at Jerusalem...*" In other words, she tested his wisdom to see if he truly understood the ancient mysteries, the *dark sayings*.

Solomon was considered wise because he was well versed in the ancient mystical knowledge. He understood the mysteries and knew how to apply them to life's situations. He was an adept, a master of the mysteries.

Queen Sheba came to test him, to discover if he truly was learnt in the **dark saying**. To discover if he was skilled in the ancient wisdom teachings passed on from generation to generation throughout the ages.

Did he possess the alchemical knowledge and was he able to make full use of its mystical, magical power? Was he truly able to perform the art of transmutation? Could he turn base elements into gold? That was the main purpose of her journey. She was not a giddy headed maiden there to seek some physical union. No. She herself was a mystic and wanted to know if this king was a fellow adept.

CHAPTER
4

The Serpent Revealer

Paul's Answer To The Dilemma

Paul in Galatians 4, reveals to us the true nature of the biblical stories. He writes:

[22] *"...Abraham had two sons, the one by a bond maid, the other by a free woman.* [23] *But he who was of the bondwoman was born after the flesh; but he of the free woman was by promise.* [24] *Which things are an **allegory...**"*

Paul, the apostle, is revealing to us the 'hidden knowledge'. The knowledge that the narratives of the Bible are nothing more than allegories?

What is an *allegory*? The dictionary describes an *allegory* as: '*a story, poem, or picture that can be interpreted* to reveal a hidden meaning'. Therefore, these are stories that point to hidden knowledge. The bible is NOT a history book, as some mistakenly believe. We are not reading about actual historical personalities or events.

Dark Saying

They are, what is referred to as, dark sayings transmitted down through the ages. These stories originate from ancient Egypt and beyond. Stories meant to reveal to the select few, truths that are hidden way beyond the muddled gaze of the oblivious masses.

According to Paul's revelation, those who are supposedly descendants of Father Abraham, also did not exist. It goes without saying that if there was no Abraham, then there was no Isaac; no Ishmael; no Jacob; no Joseph; etc. We are, as a result, left with no choice but to conclude that they are all allegorical. Characters used to point to greater, hidden truth.

Many rabbinic scholars agree that these individuals are merely symbolic in nature. They never steeped unto the pages of history.

The Serpent The Revealer Of Secrets

For the purpose of this study I shall focus only on the serpent and its meaning. So, the question is: What does the serpent signify? Now in Genesis Chapter 3,, we have the encounter that takes place between the woman and the serpent.

In the story, the woman is approached by the snake who inquiries about her liberty. She responds by saying that she generally considered herself to be free except that she is not allowed to partake of the tree in the center of the garden – 'the tree of knowledge'.

The serpent retorts:

"God doth know that in the day ye eat thereof, then your eyes shall be opened, and ye shall be as gods..."

So according to the serpent, if they eat of the 'fruit', two (2) things are going to happen:

1. Their eyes would be opened.
2. They would experience what it is like to live in their divine nature.

Did It Materialize?

Was the serpent's promise fulfilled? Absolutely! For the first time they 'know' that they were naked. They became awakened. No longer are they blind. They experience for the first time what it is to see with their third eye. They experience what it feels like to be illuminated.

"And the Lord God said, Behold, the man is become as one of us, knowing good and evil"

The phrase "knowing good and evil" is a merism which really indicates that they now had access to all knowledge. They had in fact become like God. They now knew or had access to all available knowledge. A fact that God acknowledged was indeed so.

The Gaining Of Gnosis

Throughout history the serpent is considered the bringer of knowledge – gnosis. What is gnosis? Gnosis is not knowledge gained through study or through the teacher passed on from another. Gnosis is the knowledge gained through inner knowing. It is tapping into the divine self, accessing knowledge that can only be gained from tapping into the higher self.

The Christ in repeating one of the *dark sayings* to his disciples, "be wise as serpents", acknowledges this. It is no surprise therefore, that the serpent (your elevated consciousness) is the one who reveals the secret – the secret of the tree of knowledge.

CHAPTER
5

Third Eye Activation In Eden

Eden Is Not A Physical Place

The serpent in the bible, as in all other ancient teachings, is symbolic. Just as there is no physical garden of Eden, so to there is no physical snake. It is really all about consciousness – your consciousness. It has absolutely nothing to do with anything outside of yourself.

The garden represents your place of comfort, your safety zone, your familiar space. Eden is the space where you are at rest, but it is also the place of no growth. You may get fat in Eden, but you will not grow. In the garden everything is familiar: friends; family; beliefs. There is no risk of rejection – you are safe. Naked but safe.

God Inside Of You

"Do you not know that you are a temple of God and that the Spirit of God dwells in you?"

As you are aware, there is a constant battle going on inside of us. We will all admit that there is this voice inside that speaks to us. It matters not if you are a theist; an agnostic; or an atheist, the voice never stops speaking. Some would suggest that there are two voices. One voice leading you to a higher plane, the other to a lower dimension.

First of all, it is important to remember that God resides inside, not outside of you. There are so many scriptures which points this out. Christ reminds us that *the kingdom of God is within* us, not outside. A kingdom is where the king (God) has dominion.

The king's rule is generally limited to the dimensions of his kingdom. Outside of his kingdom he has no power. So, God's rule is limited to us. We are the kingdom, the place where the Divine resides. There is no God outside of ourselves.

In this allegory 'God' represents the voice that wants you to be 'safe'. That voice which tells you to stay within 'your boundaries', your limitations. It reminds you of the ever-present dangers which lurk in the dark should you seek to explore all that you are. Fear is the greatest hindrance to our self-advancement: fear of the unknown; fear of what others would say; fear of failure.

Activating The Third Eye

The tree and its fruit in the center of the garden represents your Pineal Gland, also called your Third Eye. It is that which the masses are convinced is the epitome of all evil. The Pineal Gland enables us to *know* (Gnosis) and see things outside of the realm of our physical senses. It is that which enables us to connect with and activate our Divine self – *The God Within.*

22 And the Lord God said, Behold, the man is become as one of us, to know good and evil..."

The serpent brings to their awareness the Divinity concealed within them. Revealing that and it is only through the medium of the '*Third Eye*' that they can get in touch with the God within. It was only when they activated their Pineal Gland/*Third eye* that they are able to see what was obvious to others – *Their Nakedness.*

"...Who told thee that thou wast naked?"

'Good and Evil' is simply a figure of speech called a merism. A merism is the use of two contrasting words to show completeness. For example: *'he moved heaven and earth'* , or *'that is the long and short of the matter'*. What it does indicate therefore, is that they had activated the God kind of knowledge.

The Serpent

The serpent in this allegory refers to that inner voice which implores you to activate your *third eye*, your higher consciousness. It is the voice which challenges you to move out of your comfort zone, your Eden. It implores you to realize your nakedness and clothe yourself in the Divinity that you are.

Of course, you will face challenges, there will be pain, and possibly rejection. However, in the end you would experience what it is to live as the Divine being you are created to be.

CHAPTER
6

The Serpent Priests

Serpent Priests

"...What is that in thine hand? And he said, A rod.
[3] ...he said, Cast it on the ground. And he cast it
on the ground, and it became a serpent; and
Moses fled from before it..." Exodus 4:6

We have looked at the serpent as *the healer* and
the *giver of knowledge.* Now we will look at the
serpent as the essence of the priesthood. Without
evidence of the serpent one would not be deemed
qualified to be either a priest or king.

In the story of *the burning bush* Moses has a life altering, fiery encounter with his God. Here he is commissioned to be Israel's priest. His mission – to lead the people out of the bondage to their flesh and into the land of their promise. He is to guide them into their place of rest and the exaltation of their spirit. Egypt is symbolic of all that is fleshly and earthly – the physical realm.

However, in-spite of this Divine encounter Moses is not convinced that the Israelites would accept him as their priest. He needed evidence to prove to them that he was in fact the one called to do this work of deliverance.

So, God orders him to take the staff in his hand and throw it to the ground, whereupon it becomes a serpent. The question is: Why would the rod turning into a serpent, be evidence of Moses' suitability to shepherd his people? His priestly identification, so to speak.

Serpent Rising

In the burning bush experience Moses is called to a place of consecration. He is commanded to take off his shoes. Why? Because he has entered sacred grounds. Like all initiates, he must be led into the Most Holy place, the Holy of Holies.

Upon entering through the secret door of the great Spinx, he is led to a place where few will ever enter. There he encounters first hand 'The Holy One of Israel' who reveals to him the sacred mysteries.

During this Divine encounter his Pineal Gland is illuminated. Here, the initiate ascends celestial heights. He experiences the awakening of the Third Eye – *The Serpent Rising.*

The rod turning into the serpent *is symbolic of this Pineal Gland activation.* It is the evidence that Moses is now qualified to be the priest of Israel. The Levite priesthood, of whom Moses was the forerunner, were known as *the serpent priests.*

The Serpent Staff

In many ancient, and even modern, religious and spiritual practices, a person CANNOT be a priest/shaman without proof of an ancestral connection to the serpent. It was, and still is, the evidence of one's calling to serve either as a king/queen or priest.

In ancient times this was so among the Chinese, the Hindus. Also, among the Dogon, the Nyoro tribe and the Ancient Egyptians, the serpent was the primary requirement for those aspiring to the office of either king or priest.

It can be seen represented on the serpentine headdress of the Pharaoh. His connection with the serpent, giving him the authority and knowledge to lead. The staff of the priests of Egypt was also symbolic of them being imbued with the serpent's power. It is from this, that the writer of the burning bush narrative would have gotten his example.

The serpent priests are still with us today.

ABOUT THE AUTHOR

The Ainsworth Forgenie – is a Teacher; Researcher & Visionary. Laying bare the hidden knowledge for the diligent seeker.

Ainsworth's goal is to help you in the process of discovering the hidden power within. In order that you may awaken your latent God self.

In order that you may live a transformed life and thereby experience ascension and liberation.

For more you can visit the website at: Kosmicteacher.com

Ainsworth Forgenie

Made in the USA
Las Vegas, NV
28 April 2022